c·1

DATE DUE

$15.73

World Almanac Education

MEDIALOG INC
Butler, KY 41006

Exploring History through Simple Recipes

Civil War Cooking: The Union

by Susan Dosier

Consultant: Stephen E. Osman,
Media Relations Manager, Historic Fort Snelling,
Minnesota Historical Society

Blue Earth Books

an imprint of Capstone Press
Mankato, Minnesota

Blue Earth Books are published by Capstone Press
151 Good Counsel Drive, P.O. Box 669, Mankato, Minnesota 56002
http://www.capstone-press.com

Library of Congress Cataloging-in-Publication Data
Dosier, Susan.
  Civil War cooking: The Union by Susan Dosier.
  p. cm.—(Exploring history through simple recipes)
  Includes bibliographical references (p. 30) and index.
  Summary: Discusses the everyday life, cooking methods, foods, and celebrations of Union soldiers during the Civil War. Includes recipes and sidebars.
  ISBN 0-7368-0351-3
  1. Cookery, American—History Juvenile literature. 2. United States—History—Civil War, 1861-1865 Juvenile literature. [1. Cookery, American—History. 2. United States—History—Civil War, 1861-1865.] I. Title. II. Series.
TX715.D68745 2000
641.5973'09034—dc21   99-27048
                                                                          CIP

Editorial credits
Editor, Kay M. Olson; cover designer, Steve Christensen; interior designer, Heather Kindseth; illustrator, Linda Clavel; photo researchers, Kimberly Danger and Katy Kudela.

Acknowledgments
Blue Earth Books thanks the following children who helped test recipes: John Christensen, Matthew Christensen, Maerin Coughlan, Beth Goebel, Nicole Hilger, Abby Rothenbuehler, Alice Ruff, Hannah Schoof, and Molly Wandersee.

Photo credits
Corbis-Bettmann, cover; Gregg Andersen, cover (background) and recipes, 15, 19, 21, 23, 28, 29; North Wind Picture Archives, 8, 10, 14, 16-17, 19; Library of Congress, 9, 12, 13, 20, 22-23, 25, 27; Archive Photos, 11; Chicago Historical Society, 28-29.

Editor's note
Adult supervision may be needed for some recipes in this book. All recipes have been tested. Although based on historical foods, recipes have been modernized and simplified for today's young cooks.

1 2 3 4 5 6 05 04 03 02 01 00

Contents

Cooking Help

Recipes

References

Metric Conversion Guide

U.S.	Canada
¼ teaspoon	1 mL
½ teaspoon	2 mL
1 teaspoon	5 mL
1 tablespoon	15 mL
¼ cup	50 mL
⅓ cup	75 mL
½ cup	125 mL
⅔ cup	150 mL
¾ cup	175 mL
1 cup	250 mL
1 quart	1 liter
1 ounce	30 grams
2 ounces	55 grams
4 ounces	85 grams
½ pound	225 grams
1 pound	455 grams

Fahrenheit	Celsius
325 degrees	160 degrees
350 degrees	180 degrees
375 degrees	190 degrees
400 degrees	200 degrees
425 degrees	220 degrees

Kitchen Safety

1. Make sure your hair and clothes will not be in the way while you are cooking.

2. Keep a fire extinguisher in the kitchen. Never put water on a grease fire.

3. Wash your hands with soap before you start to cook. Wash your hands with soap again after you handle meat or poultry.

4. Ask an adult for help with sharp knives, the stove, the oven, and all electrical appliances.

5. Turn handles of pots and pans to the middle of the stove. A person walking by could run into handles that stick out toward the room.

6. Use dry pot holders to take dishes out of the oven.

7. Wash all fruits and vegetables.

8. Always use a clean cutting board. Wash the cutting board thoroughly after cutting meat or poultry.

9. Wipe up spills immediately.

10. Store leftovers properly. Do not leave leftovers out at room temperature for more than two hours.

Cooking Equipment

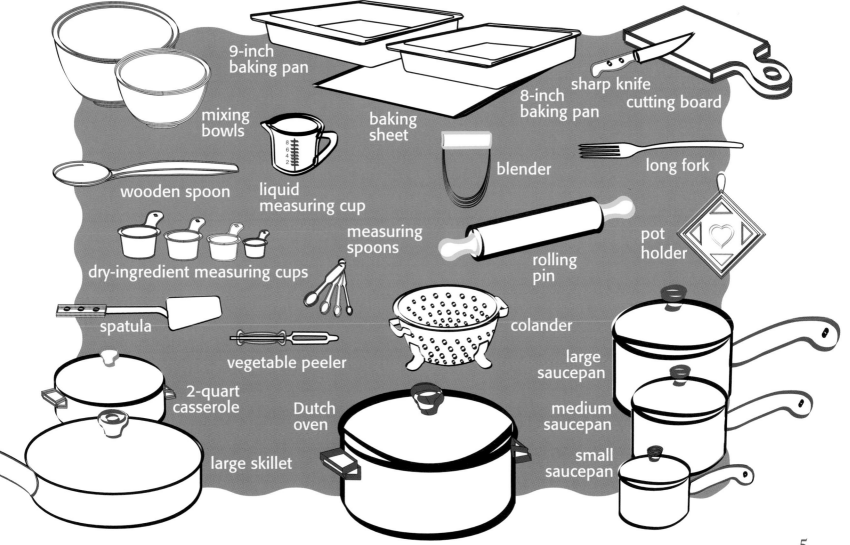

9-inch baking pan

mixing bowls

baking sheet

8-inch baking pan

sharp knife

cutting board

liquid measuring cup

blender

long fork

wooden spoon

measuring spoons

rolling pin

pot holder

dry-ingredient measuring cups

spatula

colander

large saucepan

vegetable peeler

2-quart casserole

Dutch oven

medium saucepan

large skillet

small saucepan

The Civil War

In 1860, economic differences divided the Northern and the Southern United States. Some people in the North worked on small farms. But many people owned businesses or worked in factories. Many Southerners made their living by growing cotton on large farms called plantations. These crops had to be picked by hand. Plantation owners depended on slaves to do this work.

Until the 1850s, slave traders captured West Africans and brought them to North America. These West African slaves were bought and sold as property. Some slaves were able to buy freedom for themselves and their families by paying their owners. Some people who were opposed to slavery paid owners to buy freedom for certain slaves. These former slaves were called free blacks and they lived in Northern states. Freedom for African Americans was not recognized in the South.

Northerners and Southerners disagreed about the issue of slavery. Southerners believed slavery was necessary to the survival of their farms and plantations. Northerners said Southerners did not need slavery to succeed. Some Northerners were called abolitionists. They believed slavery was wrong and should be stopped everywhere in the United States. Other Northerners thought slavery could be tolerated in the South. But most Northerners did not want slavery to be legal in western U.S. territories.

The North and South also disagreed over issues of government. Southerners believed in a strong state government. Southerners were loyal to their individual states and felt each state had the right to make laws governing social matters, including slavery. Northerners believed in a strong national government. Northerners felt political and social issues should be the federal government's business.

Abraham Lincoln won the presidential election in 1860. He was a member of the new Republican Party, which was against slavery. Many Southerners disagreed with Lincoln's political views. They began to talk about their states leaving the United States. South Carolina declared that the federal government had unlawfully taken over rights reserved for the states and became the first Southern state to secede from the Union. Ten other Southern states also left the Union within a year. These 11 states formed their own country called the Confederate States of America.

The Northern states did not want the Southern states to leave the Union. President Lincoln wanted the Union

The North and the South

1861-1865

■	Union States
□	Border States
■	Confederate States

7

to stay together. In April 1861, U.S. soldiers serving at Fort Sumter were running out of supplies. Fort Sumter was located in South Carolina, and Southerners believed the fort belonged to the Confederacy. Southerners hoped the Union soldiers would leave the fort when they faced starvation. But President Lincoln ordered federal ships to bring food and supplies to the Union troops at Fort Sumter. This action was the trigger for war.

The Civil War was the only war fought on American soil. Union soldiers were called Yankees, and Confederate soldiers were called Rebels. Yankees wore blue uniforms and Rebels wore gray uniforms. At first, both the Union and the Confederacy thought the war would end quickly. But the fighting continued for four long years. The Civil War officially ended on April 9, 1865, when the Confederacy surrendered.

Crowds cheer for Union troops as they leave for the front at the beginning of the Civil War.

Cooking

Union soldiers who lived in permanent camps or barracks did not cook for themselves. Army cooks prepared meals for these soldiers. Union soldiers who were on long marches or were fighting in battles had to do their own cooking.

Soldiers were divided into messes, whether they lived in barracks or on the battlefield. Messes were groups of four to eight men. These men ate their meals together. If they were marching, the soldiers also cooked together. The men sometimes took turns cooking. The soldier who could cook the best often made all the meals. A mess occasionally hired a free black man to cook for them.

Feeding the Soldiers

The Union Army was better able to feed its soldiers than the Confederate Army. The Union had more money and could afford to buy more food for each soldier. Because few battles were fought in the North, many of the Union's supply lines were not damaged. These open routes allowed suppliers to regularly reach the Union Army.

Although Yankees ate better than Rebels did, Union soldiers sometimes went hungry. One soldier wrote, "Some days we live first rate, and then the next, we don't have half enough."

Soldiers called the supply lines "cracker lines." This name may have come about because supply lines, like crisp crackers, often broke

Soldiers cooked and ate their meals together in groups called messes.

Union Rations

According to ration lists, the Union Army appeared to have the best-fed soldiers in the world. But the men did not get their full ration of food every day. Food sometimes was plentiful and other times was scarce for Union soldiers.

The following list shows the daily amounts of food rationed to Union soldiers from August 3, 1861, to June 20, 1864.

To each soldier:

*12 ounces of pork or bacon or 1 pound and
    4 ounces of salt beef or fresh beef*
*1 pound and 6 ounces of soft bread or flour or 1 pound
    of hard bread or 1 pound and 4 ounces of cornmeal*

For every 100 soldiers:

15 pounds of beans or peas
10 pounds of rice or hominy
*10 pounds of green coffee or 8 pounds of roasted coffee
    beans or 1 pound and 8 ounces of tea*
15 pounds of sugar
4 quarts of vinegar
3 pounds and 12 ounces of salt
4 ounces of pepper
30 pounds of potatoes
1 quart of molasses

down before food could reach the men. Dishonest supply officers sometimes sold the food instead of delivering it to the soldiers.

Early in the war, new officers did not plan well when ordering food. They ordered too much food for the soldiers to carry on long marches. Or they ordered too much of one type of food, such as fresh meat, and it spoiled before the men could eat it. Other times, new officers did not order enough food simply because they did not realize how hungry men would be after a battle.

Kitchens in army training camps were large, and cooks fed many soldiers every day. But soldiers who marched off to battle did their own cooking over campfires.

12

Water Call

A Civil War soldier needed water to drink, to make coffee or tea, to prepare and boil food, and to wash. But clean water was not always easy to find. Soldiers carried water in canteens and refilled them from wells as this photograph shows. Soldiers also drew water from rivers, lakes, ponds, or even puddles. When only muddy or dirty water was available, soldiers strained it through an old shirt or handkerchief before drinking it.

Foraging for Survival

When rations were low, soldiers often foraged for food. The countryside around the soldiers' camps provided free food for the taking. Blackberries, honey, wild cherries, apples, grapes, persimmons, and other foods often were plentiful in summer months. Soldiers who had free time between battles and work orders went foraging in the woods. They brought back fruits or berries to share or to make into tasty desserts.

Other times, foragers looking for a meal waited near a farmer's house until suppertime and then politely knocked at the door. The hungry soldiers offered some excuse for stopping and hoped that the family would set another plate or two at the table.

Union Army regulations did not allow soldiers to steal food. But officers often overlooked this rule. Foraging became necessary when soldiers were starving and needed food to survive. Soldiers might kill a stray sheep or chicken at a nearby farm. Great hunger sometimes led soldiers to steal hogs, eggs, sweet potatoes, or whatever else they could find from farms. This type of foraging was especially dangerous for Union soldiers who were marching through the South. Enemy soldiers put thieves in prison or killed them for stealing.

Hungry soldiers foraged for stray farm animals when rations were low.

Cherry Cobbler

Soldiers sometimes made fruit cobblers or pies after a successful forage in the countryside. They baked the cobbler in a covered pot in a bed of coals. The crusts of these desserts often were tough. But cobblers were still a treat.

Ingredients
2 16-ounce cans tart red cherries, drained
1 cup sugar
2 tablespoons cornstarch
¼ teaspoon ground cinnamon
1½ cups all-purpose flour
1 tablespoon butter for greasing
¾ teaspoon salt
½ cup shortening
5 tablespoons cold water

Equipment
medium saucepan
dry-ingredient measuring cups
measuring spoons
wooden spoon
8-inch by 8-inch (20-centimeter by 20-centimeter) baking dish
large mixing bowl
fork or pastry blender
rolling pin
knife
cutting board
paper towel or napkin for greasing

1. Combine cherries, 1 cup sugar, and 2 tablespoons cornstarch in saucepan. Let stand 10 minutes.
2. Cook over medium heat, stirring constantly, until thickened and bubbly.
3. Stir in ¼ teaspoon cinnamon.
4. Grease baking dish with 1 tablespoon butter and paper towel or napkin. Pour mixture into dish. Cool slightly.
5. Mix 1½ cups flour and ¾ teaspoon salt in bowl.
6. Cut in ½ cup shortening with a fork or pastry blender until mixture is in small clumps.
7. Add 5 tablespoons cold water, 1 tablespoon at a time, stirring with a fork until mixture forms a ball.
8. Heat oven to 375°F.
9. Lightly flour cutting board.
10. Pat dough into a circle on floured cutting board.
11. Roll dough to ⅛-inch (3-millimeter) thickness.
12. Cut dough into ½-inch-wide (12-millimeter-wide) strips. Lay strips criss-cross over cherry mixture.
13. Bake 40 minutes, until crust strips are lightly browned.

Makes 6 servings.

Making the Most of Meat

Meat was the most common source of protein for Union soldiers. Protein gave soldiers the energy needed to march and fight. Most soldiers craved fresh beef. But fresh beef usually was not part of their rations. Supply wagons could not keep the meat cold until it reached the soldiers. Soldiers sometimes slaughtered cattle near the camps, and they enjoyed a rare taste of roasted beef.

Army rations usually included pickled beef because it did not spoil as quickly as fresh meat. Pickled beef was very salty, and many soldiers did not like its taste. They called this salty beef "salt horse." Soldiers often tried to wash salt off the beef in a nearby stream before eating it.

Pork was probably the most common type of meat rationed to Union soldiers. Smoked hams and bacon did not spoil as quickly as fresh meat. The high fat content of pork meat provided soldiers with lard. They fried cornmeal, potatoes, and other foods in lard.

When meat supplies were low, soldiers found other types of protein to eat. Many soldiers fished and shared, sold, or traded any extra fish to fellow soldiers.

Soldiers often searched forests for food. Wild game like possum and squirrel provided protein for soldiers when other meat was scarce. Some soldiers fighting in the South foraged for wild peanuts to add protein to their meals.

Chickens and eggs were another good source of protein for soldiers. Soldiers traded, bought, and sometimes even stole chickens and eggs from nearby farms. Soldiers fried eggs in pork lard. Soldiers also hard boiled eggs and carried them in their pockets to eat during marches. Soldiers sometimes roasted eggs by standing them on end in hot campfire ashes.

When soldiers had the opportunity, they slaughtered cattle near the camp and enjoyed a meal of fresh-cooked beef.

Irish Stew

Soldiers saved leftover meat scraps for soups and stews. They needed only a few vegetables and a large pot to stretch leftovers into another meal.

Ingredients	**Equipment**
2 tablespoons vegetable oil	measuring spoons
1 boneless beef chuck roast (3 to 4 pounds)	Dutch oven or large saucepan
1 pound whole new potatoes	long fork
1 tablespoon salt	liquid measuring cup
1 teaspoon pepper	fork

1. Pour 2 tablespoons vegetable oil in Dutch oven or saucepan, warm over medium heat.
2. Add beef chuck roast. Cook just until meat is brown on all sides.
3. Add potatoes, 1 tablespoon salt, and 1 teaspoon pepper.
4. Cover with 8 cups water. Bring to a boil over medium-high heat. Reduce heat to medium. Cook 2 to 2½ hours or until meat is tender and easy to cut.
5. Place meat on platter.
6. Remove 2 potatoes with fork. Mash these potatoes with fork and stir mashed potatoes into the stew mixture to thicken the gravy.

Makes 6-8 servings.

17

Breads without Baking

Union soldiers received rations to make their own bread. But baking equipment was too heavy to be carried by foot soldiers. Instead of baking ovens, soldiers carried a cast iron pan with a lid and three short legs. This pan was called a spider. Soldiers could make biscuits and pancakes in a spider. Union soldiers also cooked johnnycakes in spiders. Soldiers needed few ingredients and very little skill to cook this type of cornbread.

Hardtack is one food most often associated with the Civil War. This hard, thick cracker was made with flour, water, and salt. Hardtack was made extremely hard on purpose. Hardtack did not break up into crumbs like ordinary crackers. Hardtack was lightweight, easy to carry, and lasted a long time without spoiling.

"... The hardtack is so precious now that the orderly sergeant no longer knocks a box open and lets every man help himself, but he stands right over the box and counts the number of tacks he gives to every man...And that ain't all. The boys will stand around until the box is emptied, and then they will pick up the fragments that have fallen to the ground...and scrape off the mud with their knives and eat the little pieces and glad to get them."

—an Illinois soldier in Jackson, Tennessee, 1862

Although hardtack did not spoil easily, it often had worms living in the holes and cracks. For this reason, soldiers gave hardtack the name "worm castle." When their stomachs were empty and there was nothing else on hand, however, soldiers ate the wormy hardtack anyway. One Union soldier said, "Hard crackers go pretty well when a person is real hungry."

Johnnycakes

People across the United States have eaten johnnycakes since the 1600s. Johnnycakes are especially popular in the northeastern United States.

Union soldiers used a cooking pan called a spider. This cast iron pan had three short legs.

Ingredients
1 cup water
1½ cups ground yellow cornmeal
½ teaspoon salt
½ cup milk
2 tablespoons butter
molasses, or syrup and butter
  for serving

Equipment
small saucepan
liquid measuring cup
large mixing bowl
dry-ingredient measuring cups
measuring spoons
wooden spoon
large skillet
spatula

1. Bring 1 cup water to boil in saucepan.
2. Combine 1½ cups cornmeal, ½ teaspoon salt, 1 cup boiled water, and ½ cup milk in bowl. Stir well.
3. Melt 2 tablespoons butter in skillet over medium heat.
4. Pour 1 tablespoon of batter into skillet. Cook over medium heat 4 to 5 minutes on each side. Cook until edges are lacy and lightly browned. Turn gently with spatula.
5. Serve hot with molasses, or maple syrup and butter.

Makes about 15 johnnycakes.

Beans Three Times a Day

Civil War soldiers ate more beans than any other vegetable. Dried beans were lightweight. Soldiers carried them on marches from battle to battle. They sometimes ate kidney beans, navy beans, butter beans, pea beans, pinto beans, or wax beans three times a day.

Union soldiers cooked beans in many ways. In the evenings, soldiers sometimes dug a little hole and built a fire in it. They then covered their pot of beans, put it in the hole, and let the beans cook through the night. Soldiers also added beans to soup. Yankees seasoned their soup with salt pork. The salt pork made the beans tastier and helped to fill the soldiers' stomachs. Any fresh or dried vegetables or greens that were available also went into the soup.

This Union officers' mess was photographed near Meade, Virginia, in 1863.

Potatoes were another important vegetable in a soldier's diet. Potatoes did not spoil as quickly as other fresh vegetables. In winter, Union soldiers received dried potatoes in their rations. Soldiers did not like dried potatoes at first, but they willingly ate them when they were hungry.

Navy Bean Soup

The beans in this recipe must first be soaked in water overnight.

Ingredients

8 ounces (1 cup) dried navy beans
5 cups water
½ pound salt pork
2 large carrots (1 cup chopped)
1 large onion (¾ cup chopped)
1 large potato, unpeeled, cut into
  ½-inch (1.3-centimeter) pieces
1 teaspoon salt
½ teaspoon pepper

Equipment

colander
Dutch oven with lid
  (or large saucepan)
liquid measuring cup
cutting board
sharp knife
vegetable peeler
wooden spoon
measuring spoons
fork

1. Wash beans in colander. Discard any discolored beans.
2. Place beans in Dutch oven or saucepan. Cover with water 2 inches (5 centimeters) above beans.
3. Soak beans overnight.
4. Drain beans in colander. Return beans to Dutch oven or saucepan.
5. Add 5 cups water.
6. Cut criss-cross pattern into salt pork with fork. Add salt pork to beans.
7. Remove skin from onion. Chop onion.
8. Peel 2 carrots with vegetable peeler. Chop carrots.
9. Stir in chopped onions and chopped carrots.
10. Bring to a boil. Cover, reduce heat, and simmer 45 minutes or until beans are tender.
11. Cut potato into ½-inch (1.3-centimeter) pieces. Add potato pieces, 1 teaspoon salt, and ½ teaspoon pepper.
12. Bring to a boil. Cover. Cook 15 minutes or until potato pieces are tender.

Makes 6-8 servings.

Dried and Fresh Fruits

Forests and farms provided fresh fruits for soldiers in the summer and autumn months. Union soldiers often picked wild berries during the summer. Union soldiers who camped in the South paid for or helped themselves to peaches, watermelons, and other fruits from nearby farms and gardens. Apples were plentiful from August through October in many areas.

Fresh fruit was seldom available in winter months. Soldiers often ate dried apples. In the fall, soldiers cut thin slices of fresh apples and let them dry in the sun. Apples dried this way did not spoil or become rotten. In winter, soldiers soaked dried apples in water, which made the slices look like fresh apples. They then fried the apples and spooned them into a pie crust to make a sweet dessert.

Dried apples provided vitamin C to the soldiers. Vitamin C prevented scurvy, a disease that makes the gums around a person's teeth bleed. Army hospitals sometimes distributed dried apples to the soldiers to keep them healthy.

The Sutler's tent was a common sight in Civil War camps. Sutlers sold items to soldiers that were not available anywhere else.

Sutlers

Sutlers were salesmen who traveled along with the soldiers. Sutlers offered items that soldiers could not get anywhere else. Sutlers usually charged high prices for their goods. They took a great deal of risk living so near the Civil War battles. Sutlers had to bring goods from long distances to reach Union troops. The prices they charged for items helped pay for their transportation.

Food, beverages, and tobacco were big sellers for Sutlers. They also sold cooking pots and pans, nails to repair boot heels, and special foods such as fresh fruits, cakes, pies, butter, and cheese.

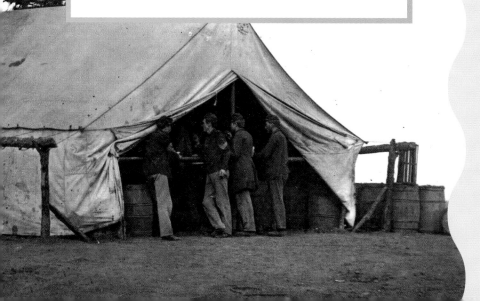

Skillet-Fried Apples

Ingredients
5 Granny Smith or other cooking apples, unpeeled
4 tablespoons or more butter
½ cup brown sugar
½ teaspoon nutmeg

Equipment
cutting board
sharp knife
large skillet with lid
wooden spoon
dry-ingredient measuring cups
measuring spoons

1. Wash apples. Remove the core and seeds, but do not peel. Cut apples into 16 narrow wedges.
2. In skillet, melt butter over medium heat.
3. Add apples. Cover. Cook 5 minutes.
4. Add 4 tablespoons brown sugar and ½ teaspoon nutmeg. Stir well.
5. Cook covered 10 to 12 minutes or until apples are tender. Check apples every few minutes during cooking. Add extra butter if needed to keep apples from sticking.

Makes 6 to 8 servings.

Life Back Home

L ife in the North did not change much for those who were rich before the Civil War began. Wealthy people made even more money by selling food, clothing, and weapons to the Union Army.

Northerners could still find fancy food and clothes to buy. They still attended parties and dances. Yankee boys often dressed in clothes that looked like Union Army uniforms.

Life changed more for Northerners who did not have much money. Work wages decreased during the war years, but costs for food and living expenses increased. Food prices rose as much as 75 percent during the Civil War. A pound of sugar that might have sold for 25 cents in 1861 was likely to cost $1.80 in 1865. Union families could not afford to buy many food items during the war. Like Union soldiers, regular citizens often went hungry.

People had to take on extra work to survive. Women took over much of the hard labor when the men in their families left to become soldiers. In winter, women had to shovel coal into furnaces to heat their homes. They had to climb up ladders to repair leaky roofs when it rained. Children had to take on more chores while their mothers were working. Young boys hauled livestock to slaughter houses so soldiers would have meat. Boys sawed firewood for their mothers, their neighbors, and sometimes even soldiers at nearby camps. Young boys living on farms took care of the animals and crops. Girls helped their mothers by taking care of younger children. They knit socks for the soldiers and made towels and bandages. Girls also helped tend gardens and cook for their families.

Wives and children of Union soldiers had to take on more chores at home after their husbands and fathers left for the war.

Old-Fashioned Macaroni and Cheese

Northeast and Midwest dairies supplied milk for making cheese.

Ingredients
8 ounces macaroni
2 tablespoon butter for
   greasing
2 cups milk
3½ cups (10 ounces)
   shredded Cheddar cheese
3 eggs
1 teaspoon salt
¼ teaspoon pepper

Equipment
large saucepan
colander
2-quart baking dish
mixing bowl
fork
liquid measuring cup
measuring spoons
wooden spoon
aluminum foil
paper towel or napkin

1. Cook macaroni according to package directions, omitting salt. Drain in colander.
2. Heat oven to 400°F. Use paper towel or napkin to grease baking dish with butter.
3. Put macaroni in baking dish.
4. In bowl, beat 3 eggs with a fork. Add 2 cups milk, 2½ cups cheese,1 teaspoon salt, and ¼ teaspoon pepper. Pour over macaroni. Stir to combine mixture with macaroni.
5. Cover with foil. Bake at 400°F for 40 minutes. Uncover. Sprinkle with remaining 1 cup cheese. Bake 5 minutes or until cheese melts.

Makes 8 servings.

The Union at Christmas

Christmas was the most widely celebrated holiday for Civil War troops. Families and friends of the soldiers sent packages from home at this time of year. Most soldiers were hungry for the special holiday treats their families made at Christmas. The food they received was good, but just being remembered was more important for most homesick soldiers.

Christmas festivities back home usually were spare. Wives and children had to make do with less money while their husbands and fathers were in the army. Soldiers received pay but did not always receive their money regularly. With fewer men to do the chores at home, families did not have as much time for celebrating. Most families and communities attended church services together on Christmas Day. They offered special prayers for the soldiers and for the war to come to an end.

"Dear Father and Mother, A Happy Christmas and Happy New Year to you. I am still alive and kicking. Today passes off without much ado ..." Albert Shaw of the 23rd Indiana Volunteers Infantry Regiment in a letter to his parents dated December 25, 1861

Union families celebrated Christmas with special meals. New Englanders ate roast turkey with stuffing. Near the coast, family Christmas menus featured crab and other seafood. Cooks made stuffing with fresh oysters. In the Midwest, families ate pork chops or hams at the Christmas dinner table. Winter vegetables such as potatoes, turnips, parsnips, and rutabagas served as side dishes. Cooks used cranberries and dried fruits in sauces and desserts.

Special cakes and candies were an important part of Christmas celebrations during the Civil War. After the first year of the Civil War, sugar and butter became scarce. Northern families saved these ingredients to bake cookies, gingerbread, and other treats for special occasions like Christmas.

Union soldiers eat a meal at their winter quarters at Brandy Station, Virginia.

Tea Cake Cookies

Cookies were a popular treat in packages sent to soldiers. Small, flat cookies were easy to pack.

Ingredients
1 tablespoon butter for greasing
5 cups all-purpose flour
1 teaspoon baking soda
½ teaspoon ground nutmeg
1 cup (2 sticks) butter
1 cup buttermilk (or 1 cup milk plus
   1 tablespoon vinegar)
2 large eggs
2 cups sugar
additional flour, if needed

Equipment
baking sheet
large mixing bowl
dry-ingredient measuring cups
measuring spoons
fork or pastry blender
medium mixing bowl
liquid measuring cup
wooden spoon
pot holders
paper towel or napkin

1. Heat oven to 375°F. Use paper towel or napkin to grease baking sheet with butter.
2. Combine 5 cups flour, 1 teaspoon baking soda, and ½ teaspoon nutmeg in large bowl. Cut in 2 sticks butter with fork or pastry blender until mixture looks like coarse crumbs.
3. In medium bowl, stir together 1 cup milk, 2 eggs, and 2 cups sugar. Pour into dry ingredients. Stir well. Wash hands, then lightly coat fingertips with butter. Shape dough into 1-inch balls. (If mixture is too wet to roll, add ½ cup additional flour and try again.) Place balls on baking sheets.
4. Dip fork in flour, then use it to flatten balls. Bake 10 to 12 minutes or until golden brown.

Makes 5 dozen cookies.

Soldiers eagerly opened boxes from home. The men most always found socks, soap, and food inside the packages.

Gingerbread

Ingredients

1 tablespoon butter or margarine
2½ cups all-purpose flour
1½ teaspoons baking soda
½ cup (1 stick butter, softened)
1¼ cups molasses
1 egg
1½ teaspoons cinnamon
1½ teaspoons allspice
1 cup very hot tap water

Equipment

9-inch by 9-inch (23-centimeter by 23-centimeter) baking pan
large bowl
dry-ingredient measuring cups
measuring spoons
wooden spoon
fork
liquid measuring cup
wooden toothpick
pot holders
paper towel or napkin

1. Preheat oven to 350°F. Use paper towel or napkin to grease baking pan with butter or margarine.
2. In large bowl, combine flour and baking soda. Cut soft butter into flour mixture with fork.
3. Add molasses, egg, cinnamon, allspice, and water. Stir well.
4. Pour batter into baking pan. Bake 35 to 40 minutes, or until wooden toothpick inserted near the center comes out clean.

Makes 9 servings.

Words to Know

abolitionist (ab-uh-LISH-uh-nist)—a member of the anti-slavery movement

barracks (BA-ruhks)—a building where soldiers live

canteen (kan-TEEN)—a small portable metal container for holding water or other liquids

cobbler (KOB-lur)—a fruit dessert with a top crust

cornmeal (KORN-meel)—ground corn

persimmon (pur-SIM-uhn)—an orange-red plum-shaped fruit that is sweet and soft when ripe

plantation (plan-TAY-shun)—a large farm found in warm climates where crops such as cotton are grown

protein (PROH-teen)—a substance found in all living plant and animal cells; foods such as meat, cheese, eggs, beans, and fish are sources of protein.

ration (RASH-uhn)—a limited amount or share of something, especially of food

scurvy (SKUR-vee)—a disease that causes bleeding gums and physical weakness; scurvy is caused by lack of vitamin C in a person's diet.

secede (si-SEED)—to formally withdraw from a group or an organization, often to form another organization

spider (SPYE-dur)—an iron skillet with three legs

sutler (SUT-lur)—a salesman who traveled along with soldiers; sutlers sold hard-to-find foods and supplies to soldiers, sometimes at very high prices.

To Learn More

Bircher, William. *A Civil War Drummer Boy: The Diary of William Bircher, 1861-1865.* Edited by Shelley Swanson Sateren. Diaries, Letters, and Memoirs. Mankato, Minn.: Blue Earth Books, 2000.

King, David C. *Civil War Days: Discover the past with exciting projects, games, activities, and recipes.* New York: John Wiley & Sons, Inc., 1999.

Sandler, Martin W. *Civil War.* New York: HarperCollins Publishers, 1996.

Segal, Justin. *Civil War Almanac.* Chicago: Lowell House Juvenile, 1997.

Wroble, Lisa A. *Kids during the American Civil War.* Kids throughout History. New York: PowerKids Press, 1997.

Places to Write and Visit

Antietam National Battlefield
P.O. Box 158
Route 65
Sharpsburg, MD 21782

Camp Dennison
7509 Glendale Milford Road
Camp Dennison, OH 45111

Drum Barracks Civil War Museum
1052 Banning Boulevard
Wilmington, CA 90744

Gettysburg National Military Park
97 Taneytown Road
Gettysburg, PA 17325

Grand Army of the Republic
Civil War Museum and Library
4278 Griscom Street
Philadelphia, PA 19124-3954

Internet Sites

Civil War Cookbook
http://almshouse.com/cookbook.htm

Civil War in Miniature
http://www.civilwarmini.com

Mason-Dixon Line Civil War Recipes
http://www.geocities.com/Pentagon/Barracks/
1369/more_recipes.html

Recipes from the Pequot Mess
http://world.std.com/~ata/recipes.htm

Index